The Spirit of Christmas Past

The Spirit of Christmas Past

LINDA CLEMENTS

SMITHMARK

This edition published in 1996 by SMITHMARK Publishers, a division
of U.S. Media Holdings, Inc., 16 East 32nd Street, New York, NY
10016.

SMITHMARK books are available for bulk purchase for sales promo-
tion and premium use. For details write or call the manager of special
sales, SMITHMARK Publishers, 16 East 32nd Street, New York, NY
10016; (212) 532-6600.

This book was designed and produced by Todtri Productions Limited
P.O. Box 572, New York, NY 10116-0572 FAX: (212) 279-1241

Printed and bound in Singapore

Library of Congress Catalog Card Number 96-68019

ISBN 0-7651-9945-9

Author: Linda Clements

Publisher: Robert M. Tod
Designer and Art Director: Ron Pickless
Editor: Nicolas Wright
Typeset and DTP: Blanc Verso/UK

CONTENTS

INTRODUCTION

Christmas is a time of fun and feasting, happiness and holidays, and it is almost impossible to imagine it other than the way we celebrate it today. The twelve days of Christmas mean decorating a tree, sending cards by the dozen, expecting Father Christmas loaded with presents, over-decorating the house with evergreens and tinsel, pulling crackers, and eating turkey, sticky puddings and iced cake by the pound. Yet many of the features that characterize Christmas for us, that feel so traditional and so ancient, are actually quite new, having existed or been developed for only about 150 years.

It seems hard to imagine that before Queen Victoria's reign (1837–1901) Christmas had little significance. It was hardly celebrated and was regarded as little more than a half-forgotten festival. We have the Victorians to thank for breathing new life into it and for transforming it into one of the most exciting times of the year. They did not invent Christmas, of course. They took the hotchpotch that it was, nurtured it and turned it into a wonderful, fun-filled family jamboree. It became a time for closeness with family and friends, for goodwill towards all and for generosity towards those less fortunate.

A Victorian Christmas is, for many people, the way Christmas ought to be. It is so easy to imagine a log fire blazing in the hearth, cards on the mantelpiece, carol singers at the door and family and friends calling around. We can see children excitedly admiring a tree glittering with lights and surrounded with presents, a house filled with beautiful decorations and a table groaning with food and drink. Many wish for snow, too, just to add icing to the rich cake that is Christmas.

Too often today, however, Christmas is an expensive, commercial affair, too long in coming and over too soon. The emphasis seems to be more and more on promoting and marketing Christmas, and many people feel that much is being lost in this process. Every year we wish it was something different, something *better*. This book is for those who wish to recapture the magical spirit of Christmas past, to celebrate the occasion with innocent fun rather as the Victorians did.

This nostalgic, evocative look at Christmas discovers the origins of the festival and how it has evolved over the centuries. Like most cultural and religious expressions, it has grown and become more complex over the years. There is a close look at some of the most enduring customs and traditions and how they arose. (Have you wassailed your fruit trees yet or dragged in your yule-log?) The role that the Victorians played in shaping the Christmas we know today is described in detail, showing how homes and Christmas trees have been decorated in the past. Knowing more about the history and meaning behind present and card-giving helps rediscover the joys involved, and finding out what feasting took place and which games and pastimes were enjoyed makes us all the more keen to re-sample such pleasures. Celebrating Christmas should be a personal and meaningful experience, and there are plenty of ideas here for those seeking a simpler, honest and more traditional way to celebrate Christmas. The magic is there, waiting to be rediscovered; just peel off the gaudy wrapping paper and find the gift of Christmas within.

CHRISTMAS LONG PAST

The story of Christmas is a fascinating one, a wonderful mélange of historic occasion and colourful customs spanning many centuries. Midwinter festivals occurred long before the Christian celebration of the birth of Christ, of course. Most civilizations have tried to survive the cold, infertile days of winter by courting the goodwill of their gods and by praying for a renewal of light and warmth.

Opposite: The very human story behind the birth of Jesus Christ has yielded many enduring religious images. This picture shows Mary and Joseph searching for a place to stay in over-crowded Bethlehem.

THE ORIGINS OF CHRISTMAS

For the Romans these midwinter festivities centred on honouring their god Saturn during the Saturnalia in late December. This period featured a great deal of drinking and making merry, the giving of small tokens and the decorating of households with evergreens. It was also customary for masters and slaves to exchange, temporarily, their garb and roles. The Roman feast of Brumalia, the birthday of the Unconquered Sun, also occurred in late winter, on 22 December. This was the religious equivalent of Christmas for those worshipping the sun-god Mithras. The Romans also celebrated the new year with a feast called *Kalendae Januarii*, which was associated with Juvenalia, a festival honouring childhood and youth.

Races such as the Celts and Vikings also had their winter solstice celebrations to propitiate the gods and ensure the return of life to the land. Throughout northern Europe this festival was called yuletide. It was a time to celebrate the annual triumph of light over darkness, to practise

"And she brought forth her firstborn son and wrapped him up in swaddling clothes and laid him in a manger; because there was no room for them in the inn." (Luke 2 : 7)

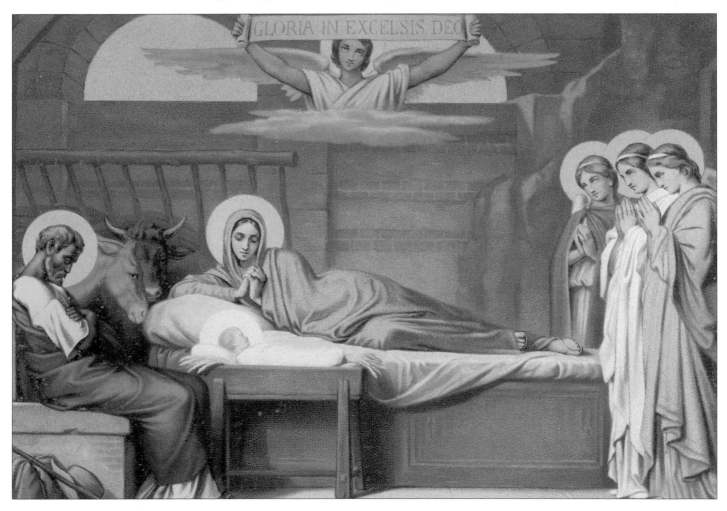

fertility rites and to burn huge fires in honour of the sun and the god Thor. As with the Romans, the festival featured much feasting and "wassailing" or toasting around the yule-log.

The Jewish people also celebrated their faith in late December, and still do, with the Feast of Lights called Hanukkah or Chanukah. For eight days candles are lit – first one, then two, then three and so on, to symbolize the strength of the faith. Gifts are given and games played during this time.

The early Christian church wanted a midwinter date to honour the birth of Jesus Christ, and in the fourth century 25 December was chosen, although, of course, this was not the true date of the nativity. This convenient date was arrived at by rather simplistically adding nine months to the official date of the Annunciation of the Virgin Mary on 25 March. The church decided that the twelve days of Christmas between the nativity and Epiphany was to be a sacred but also a festive season. Sensibly the Roman church assimilated some of the pagan customs already in existence rather than trying to eliminate them.

CHRISTMAS IN THE MIDDLE AGES

As a religious and cultural festival Christmas developed over the centuries. Throughout the twelfth, thirteenth, fourteenth and fifteenth centuries part of the celebrations included the appointment of a Lord of Misrule, who was supposed to ensure continuous fun from All-Hallows Eve on 31 October until Candlemas on 2 February. The Lord of Misrule – who was also known as the Christmas King and the Abbot of Unreason –

Early tribal peoples such as the Celts would have held midwinter celebrations to beg favour of their gods and pray for a speedy return to the light, warmth and growth of the spring and summer. This imaginary scene at Stonehenge in southern Britain shows the Celtic priesthood or learned class, the Druids, indulging in these pagan rites.

Opposite: This charming portrayal of the Nativity by an unknown artist, showing the adoration of the Christ child, reflects the peaceful spirituality of the event.

The court of Elizabeth I (1533–1603) would have been enlivened by the flamboyant figure of the Lord of Misrule. Attended by a boisterous mock court, this medieval character emerged during midwinter and personified disorder and merrymaking, turning end-of-winter festivities into an orgy of feasting, drinking, gambling and misbehaviour.

was a flamboyant figure with a mock court, and he personified enjoyment and merrymaking. Many of the antics of the Lord of Misrule were derived from the Roman end-of-year celebrations. The emphasis was on disorder, role-swapping and parody, particularly of church officials and rituals. This swayed the festivities towards an orgy of drinking, eating, gambling and general misbehaviour. During the reign of Elizabeth I (1558–1603) the Lords of Misrule made themselves unpopular with church reformers by disrupting ecclesiastical services by leading their unruly "courts" into churches and wearing fanciful clothes and grotesque masks.

THE MUMMERS PLAY

The mummers play was a medieval folk drama with much pagan symbolism that was performed during the winter months, traditionally between All-Hallows Eve on 31 October and Easter. It became a popular part of Christmas celebrations. The derivation of the word "mummer" is uncertain. It is thought to come either from the German word *mumme*, meaning mask or masker, or from the Greek word *momme*, which

means a frightening mask or ogress.

The plays were performed only by men, usually about eight, and all the characters wore disguises and masks to hide their true identities. Faces were often blackened and "visors" worn; made of fringed cloth to keep the wearer's identity secret and thus avoid losing the luck that the performance brought.

A mummers play basically dealt with the symbolic death of the earth by winter and its rebirth in the spring. In general, the characters in a mummers play were given well-known names and roles – for example, the hero might be Saint or King George and the villain would be a Turkish knight. In a typical story the scene would first be set by a rather pagan Father Christmas, who would shout and wield a club. Then the hero would arrive and be confronted by the villain. A fight would follow, during which the hero would "kill" the villain (as the plants and crops are killed by the cold season). The chivalrous hero would regret this death and eventually, after many sub-plots and general goings-on, a doctor would revive the dead man (just as the soil is rejuvenated by the sun's warmth and light in the spring).

A mummer's play, performed during the winter months in medieval times, resembled a Bacchanalian feast rather than a piece of theatre. The plays, performed by masked men, were very popular at Christmas-time and celebrated the coming end to winter. By rowdy and chaotic means the players enacted the symbolic death of the earth by winter and its welcome rebirth in the spring.

H·M·BROCK

A SEVENTEENTH-CENTURY CHRISTMAS

The seventeenth century was not a good time for Christmas – it was, to all intents and purposes, abolished thanks to the puritanical regime of Oliver Cromwell. The Puritans regarded any wild and jolly time almost as blasphemous, and Christmas, with its pagan associations, was particularly so. The election of a Lord of Misrule was, of course, forbidden, for the antics of such an irreverent character was totally unacceptable to the Puritans. In fact, an act of 1652 strictly forbade the observance of Christmas celebrations, churches were locked and shops were required to stay open. Soldiers enforced the law, and anyone found celebrating Christmas, including priests, were arrested and imprisoned. People still celebrated of course but privately and carefully.

Christmas was officially restored, along with Charles II and the monarchy, in 1660, but although the anti-Christmas laws were repealed, much of the vitality and joyousness of the occasion was lost, including the tradition of singing carols, and it did not reappear until the Victorians revitalized it in the mid-nineteenth century. Changes in society, from a rural economy to an increasingly industrial one, meant that people were moving away from the land and the hub of the country house into the cities. In the process, many of the seasonal traditions were forgotten and lost.

Many pagan midwinter customs were incorporated by the Roman church, among them the gathering of certain plants which had mystic significance. Holly was important in Christian symbolism, representing Christ's crown of thorns. Mistletoe, however, retained its pagan associations and was regarded as an evil plant, despite its reputed ability to heal maladies and ward off bad spirits. It was gathered from the woods with much ceremony by ancient peoples.

Opposite: A role-swapping custom between master and servant was in existence as early as Roman times, during the feast of Saturnalia which took place in late December each year. The practice was kept alive through the Middle Ages via the antics of the Lord of Misrule and his court. This early eighteenth-century lord continues the custom by entertaining his tenants as part of the Christmas festivities.

THE
BIRTH OF
CHRISTMAS
TODAY

Christmas today would probably be a very different occasion but for the Victorians. The Puritan rejection of the festival, although short-lived, was successful in that it changed forever the medieval idea of Christmas. Hugely sumptuous feasts, exciting tournaments, good fellowship, playing the fool and gambling were never fully revived. When Queen Victoria came to the throne in 1837, Christmas, at best a social event where neighbours and communities came together, had deteriorated to a little-remembered occasion. People did not regard the occasion as anything special or noteworthy, and they continued to work throughout. Shops stayed open, and daily papers were printed.

Yet Christmas offered everything that the socially and family-conscious Victorians could desire. All the ingredients were there – strong family feeling, piety, sentimentality, alms-giving, fun and games, feasting and drinking – they just needed to be revived and mixed in the right way, with a few new things added. The German custom of decorating a fir tree was imported to Britain and popularized by Victoria and, especially, her husband, Prince Albert. Father Christmas, metamorphosed from St Nicholas, arrived, laden with gifts, and was then transformed into Santa Claus by the Americans. The Christmas card was invented. Singing carols regained popularity. Turkey took over from beef and goose as the centrepiece of the

Opposite: The Victorian revival of Christmas was in part due to the nostalgic and evocative writings of Charles Dickens. His A Christmas Carol was hugely successful, being filled with all the right ingredients to spark a love of Christmas – ghosts, goose, plum pudding, misers, charity and salvation.

There is little doubt that Queen Victoria and her husband, Prince Albert, established Christmas as we know it today. For them, whether riding with their children in the grounds of Balmoral Castle or gathered around the Christmas tree at Windsor, it was a very special occasion – a time for family, fun and games, feasting, and charity to those less fortunate.

Queen Victoria and Prince Albert were excessively fond of their nine children and their earnest desire to temporarily halt busy state duties and spend fun time as a family was probably a major factor in the revival of Christmas as a meaningful festival. The royal family's "Christmas at Windsor", was quickly adopted as a model by their loyal subjects.

Christmas feast. Crackers and board games were invented, and many industries sprang up to produce all the presents and novelties required.

The Victorians drew all these elements together, popularized them and commercialized them, and by the time Queen Victoria died sixty-four years later, Christmas was a very different and very special occasion. It had been re-shaped into a hugely popular religious and, more importantly, a family festival centred on the hearth and home. It became a holiday to be eagerly looked forward to and long prepared for.

THE INFLUENCE OF VICTORIA AND ALBERT

The most significant change that the Victorians made was the wholesale way in which Christmas was celebrated – for the first time it was presented as a complete package. It became a time of social conscience and, most importantly, an occasion for the whole family. This change was largely brought about by the queen and prince themselves, for the family was

During the Victorian era, Christmas once again became a time of whole-hearted celebration. The giving of small tokens and gifts was an ancient New Year custom, practised by the Romans during their festival of the Kalends and also by other pagan peoples, such as the Vikings. The sending of Christmas cards is a much more recent practice, once again, thanks to the Victorians. Whether it is cards or presents that come through the door, the postman is always eagerly awaited at Christmas-time.

very important to them. They adored their children and saw Christmas as the ideal opportunity to set time aside from busy state duties to have fun with the family. The royal family was pictured in *The Illustrated London News* gaily gathered around their Christmas tree, and "Christmas at Windsor" became the established model for festivities throughout Britain. Where the royal family led, their loyal subjects followed. In time, Victoria and Albert's many children, marrying as they did into European royal households, took this idea of Christmas with them, and so the Victorian Christmas spread.

The Influence of Charles Dickens

Another profound effect on the public attitude to Christmas was the work of Charles Dickens. Like many others in the first half of the nineteenth century he was nostalgic for Christmas of the past, and he consciously set out to recapture this nostalgia and revive the spirit of the occasion in

Many new industries sprang up during the nineteenth century to cope with the increased desire to
give presents at Christmas. The festival became a
time of giving, not only to family and friends but
also to the poor, through the giving of alms and other
charitable works. Affluence had come to some
thanks to the industrial revolution but extreme hardship remained the lot of many. This time of giving,
of thought for those less well-off, salved many a
social and moral conscience.

Christmas was firmly established by the Victorians as a time for children. It was probably the one event in the year when families could spend time together in a spirit of pure fun and merry-making. Apart from all the excitement of decorating the Christmas tree and house, of giving and receiving presents, of attending parties, there were also the simple pleasures, such as reading a picture book together or walking in the country.

works such as *The Pickwick Papers* (1836–7). The mood he created can be felt in this short extract:

> When they were all tired of blind-man's buff, there was a great game at snap-dragon, and when fingers enough were burned with that, and all the raisins were gone, they sat down by the huge fire of blazing logs to a substantial supper, and a mighty bowl of wassail, something smaller than an ordinary wash-house copper, in which hot apples were hissing and bubbling with a rich look, and a jolly sound, that were perfectly irresistible.

"This," said Mr Pickwick, looking round him, "this is indeed, comfort."

"Our invariable custom," replied Mr Wardle. "Everybody sits down with us on Christmas Eve, as you see them now – servants and all; and here we wait, until the clock strikes twelve, to usher Christmas in, and beguile the time with forfeits and old stories. Trundle, my boy, rake up the fire."

Up flew the bright sparks in myriads as the logs were stirred. The deep red blaze sent forth a rich glow, that penetrated into the furthest corner of the room, and cast its cheerful tint on every face.

This representation of a scene in 1872 shows the London poor doing their Christmas marketing. The poor were often depicted in Christmas cards and illustrations of the era as jolly and contented – wishful thinking perhaps on the part of the more affluent members of society. This atmospheric setting seems more realistic: the weather looks cold and murky, few faces are smiling but the bustle suggests, perhaps optimistically, that most have money in their pockets.

Even the Victorians acknowledged that Christmas made "heavy demands on the purse" and although the gifts for ladies shown here appear expensive, most gifts for relations and friends were homemade, mainly by the females of the family. Various worthy magazines of the time exhorted that such handmade articles were preferable and should be dainty rather than costly, simple rather than elaborate.

This selection of "penny presents" shows the ingenuity of the Victorians in choosing Christmas gifts. It seems incredible now that such items, some beautifully made and intricately decorated, should have been available for so little money. Bibles, handkerchiefs, pincushions and writing cases were popular choices, as were glove boxes, photographic frames and coins.

Christmas with Mr Pickwick at the fictitious Dingley Dell was an extremely romanticized version of the festivities, but it is hardly surprising that people liked it and wanted more, for the reality was more often than not a stark contrast.

Victorian Britain was in the throes of industrialization and going through great social change. Although affluence and comfort had come to some, great hardship had been brought to many more. The gap between the conditions of the rich and the poor was so wide that many of the rich experienced guilt and anxiety about the fate of those less well-off. Benevolence and charity were the order of the day, and what better way to aid the poor than through the munificence of Father Christmas and the twelve days of Christmas?

The new style of Christmas, with its strong social conscience and family unity, was powerfully advertised in 1843 when *A Christmas Carol* was published. Dickens's story, filled as it was with winning ingredients, was tremendously successful. It had ghosts, holly and ivy, blazing log fires, roast goose, steaming plum pudding and bowls of punch. Through the

reformation of a cheerless miser, poverty was alleviated and a crippled boy saved. It was the perfect parable for well-off Victorians and their charitable aspirations. Some people, like George Bernard Shaw, saw the exploitation of sentiment as vulgar, but the story undoubtedly had a tremendous impact and many positive effects. For example, an American factory owner responded to the story and established a precedent by giving his workers Christmas Day off. In addition, the Poor Law Board, prompted by the spirit of the occasion, allowed extra food in workhouses on Christmas Day.

Apart from the work of Dickens, the popular press was also responsible for the wide and thorough spread of the fresh and romantic ideas about Christmas. Publications such as *Cassell's Family Magazine* reached a new mass market, and from the 1860s various magazines included Christmas features, stories, poems and pictures in their December issues.

Thus, the Victorian customs, both new and resurrected, have become our traditions today, and their attitudes to Christmas and the way it can be celebrated still provide us with inspiration.

Customs & Traditions

Christmas and New Year are rich with fascinating customs and traditions – more so, it seems, than any other time of year. The Victorians in particular valued these, tracing their history and drawing them together to form a coherent picture of Christmas. Most customs and traditions have their roots firmly in the long-distant pagan past, and these are often celebrated today with hardly any idea of how and why they arose. Many have a common thread and are observed throughout the world, varying only slightly from place to place.

Opposite: The custom of carol singing originated about seven hundred years ago in France, where simple songs bringing everyday events to vivid life were sung at feast days. Thankfully, the Victorians revived the delightful practise after its slump during the Puritan control of England in the seventeenth century.

THE YULE-LOG

Yuletide is today firmly associated with Christmas, and the bringing in and lighting of the yule-log on Christmas Eve was for centuries one of the most important customs at Christmas-time. Originally, however, yule was a pagan celebration. After the winter solstice on 21 December the days once again begin to lengthen, and the Vikings regarded yule as a time to celebrate the triumph of light over darkness with much drinking and feasting. Fertility rites were also practised in order to ensure a good harvest and high rates of fertility in the human and animal populations. Great fires were burned to honour the sun and to symbolize its survival, and large oak logs were also lit in honour of the god, Thor. It was this custom of burning a yule-log that spread throughout Europe, becoming one of the main Christmas traditions long before the Christmas tree.

In the mid-seventeenth century the custom in England was for a huge log of oak, ash, birch or pine to be taken into the house, usually dragged in with some ceremony by ivy-covered ropes. There was much toasting with wine and ale, then the yule-log was finally lit by a fragment of wood saved from the previous year's fire. It was thought to be unlucky to allow the yule fire to go out over the twelve days of Christmas.

Bringing in the yule-log was originally a pagan custom that took place during yule after the winter solstice, as the days again began to lengthen. Today we take the seasonal changes for granted but life was very different in the undeveloped societies of the past. The return of spring, and thus fertility to the land, was a crucial time. Lives depended on it. Little wonder it was celebrated with such gusto.

Singing and playing an instrument at home was a much more common pastime than it is today. The custom was particularly welcomed at Christmas-time when parties were the order of the day and performers were much in demand. Children were encouraged to have a "party piece" ready to perform.

BURNING YOUR OWN YULE-LOG

If you wish to recapture the spirit of this ancient custom and have the means in today's centrally heated world to do so, choose wood that is dry and well seasoned – ash, oak, beech and elm all burn well, as do fruit trees such as cherry, apple and pear. You may find that conifers, such as cedar and pine, spit too much, although they have a wonderfully aromatic smell. Silver birch can be burned, but it is often a little fiery and consumed too fast by the flames.

Once your yule-log is burning well, you may wish to make the most of the custom by having a family gathering to toast crumpets, marshmallows or chestnuts in front of the fire. This can be a delightfully evocative and memorable occasion, especially if it takes place in the evening by the light of the fire and candle decorations, with perhaps a few simple word games.

WASSAILING

Yet another pagan tradition surviving the Christian take-over of Christmas was wassailing. Wassail songs were originally sung at New Year

festivities to drive away evil spirits. A bowl called a wassail bowl, made of maple or ash and decorated with ribbons, contained a sort of punch made from ale, apples, sugar and spices. This was taken from household to household, and at each house the wassailers would sing to the inhabitants. The householders would then pay a small sum to take a drink from the bowl, replenishing it with some wassail of their own. Fruit trees were also sung to and their roots doused with wassail, in the hope that they would bear a good harvest in the year to come.

The word wassail, which derives from the Anglo-Saxon words *waes heil*, means "be whole", "be well" or "be healthy", and for centuries it was used

During Victorian times it was customary to sing carols outside, with the singers going from house to house, delivering boisterous renditions of old favourites such as "Good King Wenceslas", "We Three Kings" and "Oh Come, All Ye Faithful". Carols were also sung indoors, often as part of a party entertainment, with all the guests gathered round a piano.

as a toast at Christmas-time. The correct reply to the toast was "drinkhail" – a sort of "your health". The recipe for wassail, as used during the time of Charles I, was as follows:

> Take three pints of ale and six beaten eggs and boil together in a pewter pot. Add a quantity of roasted apples, sugar, crushed nutmegs, ginger and cloves and brew well. Drink while hot.

The English illustrator Kate Greenaway (1846–1901) produced many fanciful coloured drawings of child life. Such romantic and quaint images of children are still popular today, appearing not only in books but on many a Christmas card.

THE BOAR'S HEAD CEREMONY

From early Celtic and Norse times the ferocious wild boar was, not surprisingly, regarded with a mixture of fear and admiration throughout the British Isles and Europe. In Viking history a boar's head was eaten to honour not only the sun at yuletide but also the brave heroes of Valhalla. The Celts feared the animal as an agent of darkness, an idea the Christian church perpetuated. By the Middle Ages wild boar hunts had become a common sport.

The symbolism of the boar is powerful, and a boar's head has been part of Christmas dinner in grand and royal houses for many centuries. In 1898 it featured at Queen Victoria's Christmas table, presented with a lemon in its mouth and decorated with bay and rosemary. Each year a boar's head ceremony takes place at Queen's College, Oxford, on the Saturday before Christmas. This feast commemorates a student's lucky escape from a boar, when he shoved a copy of Aristotle into the animal's mouth to avoid a savaging. The boar's head is carried in to the diners to the accompaniment of a choir singing the "Boar's Head Carol".

Opposite: In the past it was never too early to learn to sing and play an instrument. Time spent as a family in such creative pursuits would amply fill the hours that we now spend watching television.

STIR-UP SUNDAY

Traditionally the Sunday before Advent was the last chance to begin the making of Christmas puddings and cakes if they were to be ready for the 25 December. It was not called Stir-up Sunday because of the culinary connotation, however, but after the Collect in the church service of that Sunday, which includes the verse:

> Stir up we beseech thee, O Lord, the wills of thy faithful people, that they plenteously bringing forth the fruit of good works; may of thee be plenteously rewarded.

CHRISTMAS CAROLS

The singing of carols has not always been a custom exclusive to Christmas-time. Carols originated in France in the late thirteenth or early fourteenth century. Initially, they were simple songs in joyful, everyday language, evoking vivid and down-to-earth images. They were sung on

Opposite: This illustration from Harper's Monthly 1873 shows the bringing in of the boar's head – all decorated with holly and with an orange or lemon stuck in its mouth. Boar was a centrepiece of the Christmas table for many centuries, along with other exotic meats such as swan and peacock.

WITH CAROL SWEET AND MERRY LAY
WE GLADLY WELCOME NEW YEAR'S DAY!

Hoping perhaps for a warm mince pie and a sip from the wassail bowl, these carol singers seem impervious to the winter weather. A scene like this, with other Christmas motifs, such as holly and robins thrown in for good measure, was a common one on Christmas cards in the late nineteenth century.

feast days, including Easter, Whitsun and Christmas, but were more often performed at large banquets and feasts and were ballads rather than religious songs. The name "carol" comes from the French meaning ring, because carollers usually danced in a ring as they sang.

During the Commonwealth and Protectorate in England (1649–60), carol singing was strictly limited, and those that were sung were plain dirges. Even after the Restoration of the monarchy in 1660, carol singing did not really regain its former popularity. It was left to the Victorians to rescue it, keen as they were to revitalize Christmas and all its joyous customs. Old carols and hymns were collected, new ones written and many books published on the subject. By the 1880s carols had become increasingly popular and were sung in churches, in the streets and at home around the piano on Christmas Eve. As in earlier times, groups of people went from house to house singing carols, receiving a mince pie and welcome drink from the wassail bowl for their efforts.

Today we still sing carols for the pure pleasure of it, and most of us know the words of at least half a dozen. Some of the most popular include "Silent Night", "O Come, All Ye Faithful", "Away in a Manger", "We Three Kings", "O Little Town of Bethlehem", "Hark! The Herald Angels Sing" and "Good King Wenceslas". There might not be as many house-to-house visits today, but organized carol concerts are probably more fun, and it is well worth attending one at Christmas-time – a particularly evocative location being a church or, better still, a candle-lit cathedral.

BOXING DAY AND CHRISTMAS BOXES

The day after Christmas Day is traditionally called Boxing Day. It is supposed to take its name from the alms boxes that were placed outside churches during the seasonal period to receive donations for the poor. The boxes were opened on Christmas Day, and the contents distributed the day after. This was called "the Box money" or "the dole of the Christmas Box".

An alternative and also long-established custom at Christmas-time was the practice of servants and apprentices being allowed to ask their masters for small donations of money during Advent. The money was usually saved in earthenware boxes, which had to be smashed to release the money. This was done after the Christmas festival was over – usually on Boxing Day – when the boxes were at their fullest.

Christmas is an ever-evolving festival and in the middle of the nineteenth century eating customs at Christmas-time underwent a major change with the arrival of the Turkey bird. The fowl, which quickly replaced beef and goose as the centrepiece of the Christmas table, was named after the Turkish merchants who introduced it to England.

A slightly more modern custom, which many people still follow, is the giving of Christmas "boxes" to people who have provided a regular service during the foregoing twelve months, such as refuse collectors, milkmen and postmen. In the last century this would also have included lamp-lighters, turncocks, parish watchmen and the like, who would be given these small gifts of money on Boxing Day. These days, this custom is more likely to be observed in the working week before Christmas.

MIDNIGHT MASS

An important tradition for practising Christians is to begin the celebration of Christmas on Christmas Eve by attending Midnight Mass. Mass is said every Sunday, of course, but Midnight Mass is somewhat special, often allowing a freer rein to the congregation than at other times and including an acceptance, if not the observance, of the more pagan side of Christmas. It is also a special time for those wishing to honour the true meaning of Christmas – the birth of Christ – providing a meaningful and thought-provoking few hours with friends and family.

In addition to the purely Christian custom of Midnight Mass, there are many superstitions about Christmas Eve. Animals, honouring the arrival of Jesus Christ, are supposed to be able to speak to humans at this time. One custom reports that evil creatures, such as witches and ghosts, are supposed to have their powers suspended during this holy time.

DECORATING THE HOUSE

Probably the cheapest, most plentiful and most natural way to decorate the house at Christmas is with evergreens. Plants such as holly, ivy, mistletoe, laurel and bay, which retain their leaves throughout the dark, dismal winter months, have long been important. As far back as pagan times they were symbols of life – a promise of renewal at a time when the trees were bare, the ground hard and cold, and the light and warmth of the sun diminished. Berried plants, such as holly, ivy and mistletoe, were particularly valued, their berries seen as a sign of fertility during the dead months of the year.

Much mystic significance and superstitious power was attached to such plants. The Romans used evergreens symbolically, particularly during the midwinter festival of Saturnalia. They decked their homes with holly and ivy to signify good fortune, and they attached boughs of laurel to their doorposts as a sign of victory. Holly was particularly important in Christian symbolism, representing not only the burning bush from which God spoke to Moses but also Christ's crown of thorns. In medieval times holly and ivy were often given male and female characteristics respectively. On a more modern note, the practice of hanging wreaths of evergreens, pine cones and nuts on the front door originally came from Scandinavia, and it is thought to denote friendship and renewal. A wreath or ring outside the house certainly looks cheerful and welcoming.

We still use evergreens to decorate our homes at Christmas. Holly, ivy, mistletoe, laurel and bay are the most often seen, with rosemary, box and

Decorating the house with evergreens is a long-established practice, with holly, ivy, mistletoe, laurel and bay being used as far back as Roman times. Garlands and wreaths make lush and welcoming decorations and the Victorians used evergreens in this manner all over the house at Christmas-time.

Opposite: Traditional Christmas decorations were those found in nature and evergreens such as holly, ivy, mistletoe, laurel and bay not only provided a vibrant, alive look to homes at a dismal time of year but also symbolized the coming renewal of life to the earth. Plants that stayed green throughout the harsh winter months, and especially those that bore fruit at this time, were naturally regarded as special.

yew being used to a lesser extent. Of course, there is nothing to stop you from adding to this list. Many modern garden plants, such as euonymus, skimmia and aucuba, have evergreen, usually brightly variegated leaves. Coupled with bold indoor plants, such as poinsettia (*Euphorbia pulcherrima*), they make gorgeous Christmas decorations, especially when fashioned into table decorations, or draped over a doorway or arranged *en masse* in a fireplace.

HOLLY

Holly (*Ilex aquifolium*) has, in the past, been credited with healing properties, curing such maladies as rheumatism, asthma and gout. It is also said to protect the home from various dangers, including thunder and lightning.

  It is usually easy to buy, although the supply may be limited to the plain green-leaved, red-berried varieties. You can cut your own, but should never do so from the wild and only from a friend or neighbour with their permission. If you do cut holly, take small bits from around the whole shrub because the plant is rather slow growing and will look odd for quite a time. Holly is easy to cultivate and is available in many forms – from plain leaf colours to startling variegations, from smooth-leaved varieties to

In many households, hanging the Christmas decorations is a family activity, though most young children will not be as adept as these little ones seem to be. Commercially made banners, baubles and mobiles have increasingly replaced natural materials and handmade decorations but evergreens can still be used to complement these. An old belief says that bringing evergreens into your house at this cold time of year will encourage sylvan spirits in, where they can survive the ravages of frost.

Opposite: The Christmas tree – another Victorian innovation – is so fundamental to our Christmas celebrations today it is hard to imagine our homes without one. Decorating the tree can be as simple as you like or taken to stylish extremes, though if the spirit of Christmas past is to be recalled then it is more meaningful and enjoyable if done with loved ones.

47

Decorating the whole house at Christmas-time, or at the very least the reception rooms, was very popular in previous centuries. The Victorians were very enthusiastic about dressing the whole house and spared no effort to make it cheerful and congenial. Mottoes of welcome were placed in the hall, a lattice-work of laurel leaves decorated bare walls, while garlands of holly and ivy were wound around pillars, over doors, up stairways and round picture frames. If the holly was short of berries, then peas dipped in red sealing wax were substituted.

ultra prickly ones. There are also hollies with different coloured berries – red, orange or yellow.

IVY

Ivy (*Hedera helix*) was also supposed to have magical properties, being thought to have the ability to drive away evil spirits. In the past it was hung in the milking shed to stop milk from souring. It also had healing properties, although of a prosaic kind, such as preventing baldness and curing corns.

Ivy is easy to grow and available in different leaf colours and sizes – plain, variegated with yellow or white splotches or red patterning. Ivy is also a quick grower compared to holly, especially the common *Hedera helix*. Decorative forms, such as *Hedera colchica* 'Dentata Variegata' or *H. c.* 'Paddy's Pride', have beautiful variegated markings, and they look particularly lovely as trailing decorations on stairways, fireplaces, tables and around picture frames.

MISTLETOE

In contrast to holly, mistletoe (*Viscum album*) was regarded as an evil plant by Christians. One myth suggests that it used to be a tree from which the wood used to make the cross of Christ was taken and that it shrank to its present size from shame. The plant was undoubtedly used in pagan, particularly Druid, rites and celebrations, and it is still largely unused in church decorations even today.

Mistletoe is a parasite that grows on a host (to which it does no harm). There are many beliefs about it – that it can ward off St Vitus dance and epilepsy, that it can protect against black magic and that it promotes peace and harmony. It is also supposed to afford protection against witch-

Opposite: This simply made frame with its gold-sprayed ivy leaves shows how evergreens can be given a more contemporary look. Such a decoration could easily be made by children, though the spray paint will need responsible handling.

To the Victorians, Christmas was a time to get together with friends and relations and welcoming them properly was a crucial part of Christmas custom. Lighting the house, including the entrance, was an important part of this welcome and allowed all the decorations to sparkle and glisten. Hazardous, though atmospheric, candle-light was largely replaced by electric lights by the end of the nineteenth century.

When your friends arrive give them a bright reception

BY USING HEARN'S LAMPS

craft, and thunder and lightning, to be a remedy against poison and to aid fertility in men.

Most people find room for at least one sprig of mistletoe at Christmastime if only as an excuse to kiss anyone who takes their fancy! It is usually freely available at Christmas, but if you have an old apple tree and are prepared to wait a couple of years you can propagate your own from seed. Simply make a cut in the bark of an old apple or other fruit tree and spread some seeds deep into the cut. Seal the wound with clay or something similar and wait. You should have mistletoe in two to three years.

Opposite: For centuries holly has been a favourite plant for decorating the house at Christmas-time. Not only does it look bright and cheerful but was, in the past, supposed to cure various ailments, such as gout and rheumatism. It was also credited with the useful ability to protect the home from hazards such as thunder and lightning.

51

These elegant ladies seem to have all the time in the world to decorate the house for Christmas but, as today, there was a lot to be done in a short space of time, particularly if the greenery was to be kept fresh for the whole of the festivities. As well as the favourites, holly, ivy and mistletoe, the Victorians would have used dried flowers and grasses, bulrushes, feathers and even stuffed birds.

DECORATING THE HOUSE WITH EVERGREENS

Evergreens can be used in any number of ways to bring festive cheer to the house. Small bunches or single sprigs can be very effective used on picture frames, as table decorations or on top of the Christmas pudding.

CHAINS AND ROPES

Evergreens made into chains or ropes are more elaborate. These can be made by sewing or stapling laurel leaves on to lengths of masking or binding tape or thin strips of fabric. These can then be used to wind round banisters or to frame doorways and windows or they can be hung across a

room, in much the same way that we use paper chains nowadays. Alternatively, a wall can be decorated in a crisscross fashion from top to bottom, creating a lattice-work of chains.

WREATHS

Door wreaths are symbols of welcome and friendship, and they are particularly appropriate in the festive season when family and friends call. An evergreen wreath is simple to create with florist's wire, which can be formed into the basic circle, and once it is woven with evergreens, it can be adorned with shiny ornaments, fruit, nuts, pine cones, ribbons and flowers – almost anything you like, in fact.

The Advent wreath was the centrepiece of Christmas celebrations before

Christmas decorations today are likely to be commercially made from artificial materials. The convenience of using such decorations cannot be denied and if you choose carefully there are some gorgeous ones available, all a-sparkle with opalescence and rich jewel-like colours. And of course, there is nothing to stop you from customizing shiny balls.

There can be fewer sights more cheerful and welcoming at Christmas-time than a ring or wreath on the front door or porch. If you do not wish to make your own from scratch, why not buy a basic one and add your own additional decorations, such as coloured baubles, trailing ribbons, pine cones, nuts and fresh flowers.

the Christmas tree became popular. It had four candles, symbolizing the Sundays in Advent, placed in a ring of evergreens and fir cones. It was usually hung from the ceiling, although it could also be displayed as a table centrepiece.

GARLANDS

Garlanding a house with evergreens is a much older tradition than the Christmas tree. A garland may frame a window and the wintery scene outside. It can look wonderfully opulent and fall in magnificent swags all the way down the staircase, or it may stretch boldly across a mantelpiece, drawing attention to a roaring fire. It may, more decorously, edge the dining table, ready to welcome Christmas revellers. As with other kinds of evergreen decoration, the effect can be enlivened by the use of more modern decorations, such as gold cherubs nestling among glittering baubles and bows.

PAPER DECORATIONS

Making paper decorations is still a very popular craft, despite dozens of plastic and metallic decorations that are commercially available. Making them with friends and family is also a wonderful way to recapture that essence of togetherness and good-will that the spirit of Christmas past had.

CHAINS AND GARLANDS

Paper chains are probably the one decoration that many of us remember best from our childhoods. They have been part of Christmas for a long time and are ideal for children to make. Pre-cut strips of gummed, multi-coloured paper can, of course, be readily bought, but you can easily make your own from wrapping paper, crêpe paper or even strips torn from the colourful pages of magazines.

BAUBLES AND MOBILES

Most of the decorations used to embellish Victorian Christmas trees were made of paper and card, and today there is scarcely a limit to ideas for making paper baubles and three-dimensional cut-outs to adorn the tree or house. Mobiles are great fun to make, and there is any number of shapes and forms that can be used to create pretty rotating decorations – snowflakes, Christmas trees, stars and moons, hearts, fruit – whatever you wish.

Samplers are embroidered pieces of fabric displaying stitching skills. They were usually stitched by girls and commonly included an alphabet, figures and names, with perhaps patterned areas. Not only was such counted thread embroidery given as gifts at Christmas-time but samplers with a festive theme would be hung as decorations.

CANDLE DECORATIONS

Christmas is the ideal time to use, give and even make candles. As a decorative feature they are hard to beat, for not only do they provide soft, warm lighting that makes the festive days more special, but they blend

Above: Using candles as decorative items at Christmas needs to be done with care. Wooden candlesticks such as these look charming but candles left burning right down to the wood could create more of a glow than you anticipated.

Left: This clever use of a mirror multiplies the delightful effect created by this candle decoration. Candles also add an interesting dimension to evergreen decorations, casting their warm glow over the glossy leaves.

Opposite: A lighted candle creates instant atmosphere, making the simplest of occasions seem special – little wonder that the Victorians initially used them with such fervour. The Christmas trees of that era are usually depicted gloriously ablaze with candle-light but in reality the practice was lethal, leading to many deaths before electric "fairy" lights superseded candles.

The cracker was invented by Thomas Smith in 1840, developed from French bon-bons which were twists of coloured paper that held sugared almonds. He added the bang by creating friction between two strips of chemically impregnated cardboard which were pulled apart.

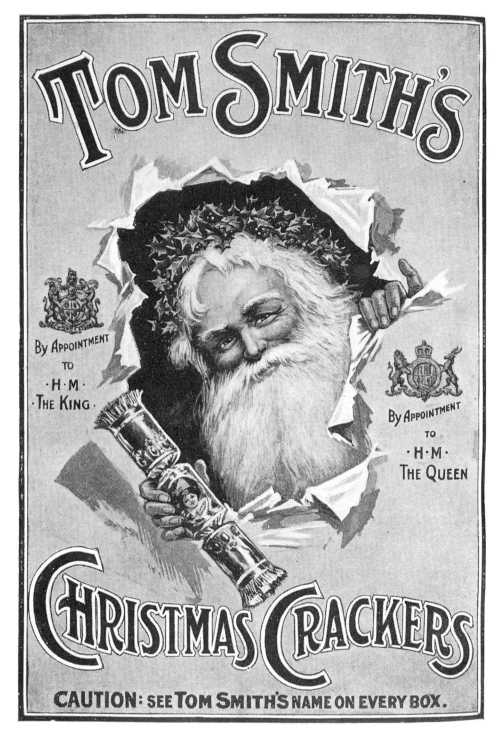

well with other decorations, particularly evergreens. Here are some simple ideas for using candles and recapturing the intimate atmosphere of Christmas gone by. (It goes without saying that extreme care should be taken with any naked flame and candles should never be left burning in an unoccupied room.)

Place a variety of candles of different heights close together on a glass cake stand, with the tallest in the centre. Decorate the edge of the stand with sprigs of holly and trailing sprigs of ivy, and use the decoration as a table centrepiece.

Another possibility is to fill a rectangular wicker basket, about 12 x 7in

(30 x 18cm) with candles, preferably ones shaped like fruits such as apples or pears. Make sure that the wicks are well above the top of the basket and that they are not positioned under the basket handle. Place the basket beside the fire – a matching pair would look good – or on a hall table.

If you are having an elegant party, place some small, floating star or flower-shaped candles in a large, decorative glass bowl to decorate a buffet table.

CRACKERS

Like many of the features of our Christmas today, the cracker is a relative newcomer: it was invented in Victorian England in 1840 by Thomas Smith, a confectioner by trade. When he was visiting Paris he noticed some *bon-bons* on sale – twists of coloured paper containing sugared almonds – and he brought the idea back to England and developed it by adding a love motto and little toys. His idea really took off when he added the "bang". He was reputedly sitting by the fire at Christmas when a log crackled loudly, and this gave him the idea for a log-shaped package containing a bon-bon, a motto and, of course, the bang!

By the end of the century crackers were being produced by the million. The contents were at times unbelievably elaborate – masks, puzzles, perfumes, musical toys, fans, hats, coats, umbrellas, eyeglasses – a far cry from the paper hat and unrecognizable plastic article found in most of today's crackers. It is possible to buy cracker-making kits, however, so if you have been disappointed with those you have bought in the past there is nothing to stop you from making your own. You can even make them in coloured paper that matches your table decorations and make sure that the trinkets and little tokens inside them are appropriate to the person who pulls each one.

THE CRIB

In Christian households a model version of the nativity scene is an important decoration. More accurately, it is a symbol of the true meaning of Christmas, and the idea dates back to the time of St Francis. The scene represents the stable in which Jesus was born, and it is particularly valuable in teaching children the meaning of Christmas. There are some very beautiful and detailed models available commercially or you may chose to make your own from simple materials.

TAKING DECORATIONS DOWN

There are lots of superstitions about when to put decorations up and perhaps even more about when to take them down. Traditionally, decorations can be put up after 6 December. Purists say it is unlucky to do this before Christmas Eve, but for many people today that's *far* too late in their busy schedules.

Epiphany (the twelfth day of Christmas – i.e., 6 January) is supposed to be the most auspicious time to take decorations down, although in the past some held out until Plough Monday (the first Monday after Twelfth Night – i.e., 8 January) or even Candlemas (2 February).

DECORATING THE CHRISTMAS TREE

THE ORIGINS OF THE CHRISTMAS TREE

Ask most people what the focal point of Christmas is for them and they will probably say the tree. It is found in almost every home in the British Isles and many other countries, but the Christmas tree is actually only about 150 years old. Charles Dickens called it "that pretty German toy", suggesting that at least before the 1850s the Christmas tree was very much a European tradition.

Many people believe that it was Prince Albert who introduced this particular form of decoration into England. It is true that he set up a tree at Windsor in 1841, wishing his children to enjoy the custom as much as he had done in his childhood. In fact, however, a fir tree was in use in this way before this, mostly in the homes of immigrant German families, although Queen Caroline had one at a children's party in 1820 and Queen Charlotte, the wife of George III, was supposed to have had a Christmas tree at Windsor as early as 1789. What Albert and Victoria did do was popularize this custom and make it fashionable. So successful were they,

A Christmas tree is always a delight to children; not only is it a visual feast they only see once a year but it is usually surrounded by exciting things – candy canes, sugared almonds, chocolate coins, nuts, fruit and, of course, presents.

Opposite: It is little wonder that a Christmas tree becomes the focal point of our decor at Christmastime. A conifer like this looks marvellous whether trimmed traditionally or in a contemporary style. The Victorians managed to load it with an amazing variety of articles – from fruit and sweets to miniature furniture and musical instruments.

In Victorian times lighting the tree by tapers usually took place for the enjoyment of children but only for a short time on a single occasion. Naked flame and dry wood were simply too hazardous a combination. Often a servant would be stationed nearby to keep watch and douse the candles that had burned too low.

Opposite: This Christmas tree lit by beautiful Chinese lanterns has the added bonus of yielding presents for children. Donating gifts to foundling children would have been the charitable thing to do during Victorian times, honouring the true spirit of the festival. Today, our practice of buying Christmas cards in which a percentage of the profits go to charities is a similar wish to help those less fortunate than ourselves.

that within twenty years it had become a practice emulated by most of their subjects.

THE KISSING BOUGH

In many rural areas of England the kissing bough predated the Christmas tree. The bough was usually a fairly rigid, spherical framework, which was decorated with evergreens. Inside the "bough" red apples were hung from coloured ribbons. Candles were placed around the circumference of the frame, with mistletoe dangling from the base. It was then hung in a prominent place to provide a focal point, much as a Christmas tree does today.

LIGHTING THE TREE

The Victorians did not have access to electric "fairy lights" until the 1890s, so in the early years lighting the tree was a take-your-life-in-your-hands candle-lit affair. Many fires were caused and many lives were lost by candles burning down, and so dangerous was the practice that a tree blazing with lights, as often shown in paintings and etchings of the mid-Victorian period, was actually a rare sight. More often than not, a tree was

Opposite: Presents, presents and more presents! Christmas morning is perhaps the best time to be a child. For Christian families this is a reminder of the true meaning of Christmas and how the three wise men from the Orient – Caspar, Balthasar and Melchior – brought gifts of gold, frankincense and myrrh to honour the birth of the baby Jesus.

Sweetmeats were very popular tree decorations in Victorian times. Apart from crunchy candy canes there would also be sugar-plums, nuts, fresh and candied fruit, chocolates and sugared almonds.

lit for only a short period on a single occasion, and usually for the children to admire.

With the invention of electricity things became much safer, and trees were illuminated by increasingly elaborate lights – some might say to the detriment of the spirit of Christmas. But whatever lighting you use, if any, it is only one way of capturing the spirit of the past. When they are thoughtfully used to enhance the other decorations on your tree, lights can create a wonderful atmosphere.

DECORATING THE TREE

Illustrations from the Victorian era show Christmas trees adorned with every possible trinket and bauble, although the great proportion were beautifully wrapped small gifts and sweetmeats. Most of the decorations were handmade, although glass balls specifically made to hang on Christmas trees started to appear later in the century.

Today our Christmas tree decorations are usually commercially made, but that does not mean they are not full of history, and they can evoke memories of Christmases past for us year after year, especially if we are fortunate enough to have some objects that have been handed down through the family. For many of us, however, tree decorations have perhaps degen-

Christmas tree decorations are myriad – no shape, size, colour or material seems out of place. These superb pieces of craftsmanship are cut from thick metal foil but you could make something similar out of silver or gold coloured paper or card.

Opposite: This charming festive scene has many of the ingredients that the Victorians introduced to Christmas – a glittering fir tree, cards standing on the mantelpiece and exciting presents strewn around.

Edible tree decorations look scrumptious but if they are the only ornaments you might find the tree is a little bare by the end of the first day!

erated to nothing more than strategically placed baubles (either far too many or nowhere near enough), some sagging and rather threadbare lengths of tinsel and perhaps a few foiled-wrapped sweets.

It does not have to be like this, however. There are many ways in which a tree can be dressed, and there is a lot of fun to be had in doing so. The following description of a Christmas tree by Charles Dickens shows just how restrained we are, with our shiny balls and pieces of tinsel.

I have been looking on, this evening, at a merry company of children assembled round that pretty German toy, a Christmas Tree. The tree was planted in the middle of a great round table, and towered high above their heads. It was brilliantly lighted by a multitude of little tapers; and everywhere sparkled and glittered with bright objects. There were rosy-cheeked dolls, hiding behind the green leaves; and there were real watches (with movable hands, at least, and an endless capacity of being wound up) dangling from innumerable twigs; there were French-polished tables, chairs, bedsteads, wardrobes, eight-day clocks, and various other articles of domestic furniture (wonderfully made, in tin, at Wolverhampton), perched among the boughs, as if in preparation for some fairy housekeeping;

Europe has a long tradition of baking special cakes, breads and biscuits for the festive season, many of which have sacramental or sacrificial significance. Markets in Germany sell a large range of decorated spiced biscuits, cakes and gingerbreads at Christmas-time, while Russians prepare pastries called "hvorost", which means branches.

there were jolly, broad-faced little men, much more agreeable in appearance than many real men – and no wonder, for their heads took off, and showed them to be full of sugar-plums; there were fiddles and drums; there were tambourines, books, work-boxes, paint-boxes, sweetmeat boxes, peep-show boxes, and all kinds of boxes; there were trinkets for the elder girls, far brighter than any grown-up gold and jewels; there were baskets and pincushions in all devices; there were guns, swords, and banners; there were witches standing in enchanted rings of pasteboard, to tell fortunes; there were teetotums, humming-tops, needle-cases, pen-wipers, smelling-bottles, conversation-cards, bouquet-holders; real fruit, made artificially dazzling with gold leaf; imitation apples, pears and walnuts, crammed with surprises; in short, as a pretty child before me, delightedly whispered to another pretty child, her bosom friend, "There was everything, and more."

Magazines are filled with ideas for decorating at Christmas-time, illustrating differing themes and colour schemes – huge tartan bows one year and tumbling dough-craft fruit the next. Whatever theme or method you choose, try to create a memorable spectacle as the Victorians did.

Below: In many European countries the Christmas tree is decorated by adults, only revealed to the children of the house in its full ornamented glory. In Britain and America the decoration of the tree tends to be a all-hands-on affair. The basic rules of decorating are: •place the tree in a spacious position, leaving room to decorate behind it; •ensure the tree is completely stable and upright in its pot and use a anti-desiccant to slow needle loss; •decorate the trunk and tub first so that fragile ornaments are not put at risk; •arrange the lights on the tree next, checking them first to ensure all bulbs work and that they are attached to a fused plug; •decorate with your ornaments from top to bottom, all the way round, avoiding concentrating just at

It is easy nowadays to dress your tree in a way that evokes these times, and you can, if you wish, like the Victorians, make your own tree decorations, using an atmospheric mix of old and new materials. Children in particular love to do this. Using nothing more elaborate than paper, cardboard, tissue paper, paper doilies, glue and perhaps a little glitter, they can see their handiwork displayed over the Christmas period. The sophistication of the effect is unimportant – what is important is the sense of family occasion, the feeling of doing things together. You may even decide to make some extra decorations and take them to a local retirement home or hospital.

❋ Cardboard (from a cereal packet) can be cut into shapes, such as stars and moons or simple fruit and bird shapes, and then either sprayed with gold or silver paint, or covered with brightly coloured paper. An extra scattering of glitter over a thin smear of clear glue will add that extra festive sparkle. Use a hole punch to pierce a hole in the top of the decorations, add a loop of cotton or ribbon so that you can hang them from the tree.

❋ Pierce a hole in a table tennis ball, then spray or paint the ball in a bright festive colour, say scarlet. When the paint is dry, spread small circles of clear glue on the ball and shake a contrasting coloured glitter – silver or gold, perhaps – over the ball. Alternatively, you could glue small "jewels" on to the ball (these are available from craft shops). Once dry, open out a paper clip into a figure-of-eight shape and push one half through the hole in the ball, then hang your bauble on the tree.

❋ Place a few sugared almonds, nuts or foil-wrapped chocolate coins in the centre of a paper lace doily. Draw the edges of the doily up and around the contents and secure at the neck with a narrow piece of Christmassy ribbon. Hang the "bon-bon" from the tree by one of the ribbon loops.

GROWING YOUR OWN CHRISTMAS TREE

If you want to grow your own tree, it is best to cultivate two and bring them in on alternate years, to prevent too frequent damage and distress to the roots. You will need to choose your conifer carefully or you could end up with a 30ft (10m) specimen in ten or fifteen years' time! Select a tree of dwarf or medium height and growth, such as one of the *Picea* or *Abies* species.

Preparing a conifer for the house is quite simple. First, dig up the tree and trim the roots. The large, anchoring roots can be cut back quite severely, with the surrounding, more fibrous root ball being trimmed more judiciously. Select a large pot, with an accompanying saucer or drip-tray, and part fill it with sand, which is a much less messy alternative to water-logged garden soil. Place the tree in the pot, spreading out the roots as well as you can, and add more sand to within about 2in (5cm) of the top of the pot. Firm down well, then water profusely and leave to drain. Spray the foliage with an anti-water loss spray before bringing the tree into the house. Once the tree has served its purpose, take it back outside. Dig over its original growing place and fork in a light scattering of fertilizer. Re-plant the tree, firm in and water well.

GIVING CARDS & PRESENTS

No one today could imagine Christmas without the giving of cards and presents, but this custom as we know it developed only during Queen Victoria's reign (1837–1901). Before then, exchanging charms and small tokens of good luck was part of the New Year celebrations. Gift-giving, like many other Christmas traditions, originally dates back to pagan and ancient Roman times – long before the midwinter feast assumed a Christian significance. Tokens of friendship and esteem were given on New Year's Day as part of the Roman festival of the Kalends. The gifts were often of honey and cakes, symbolizing the giving of sweetness for the year to come. This New Year custom of gift-giving was prevalent throughout England and much of Europe. Woden, the chief Norse god and the precursor to Father Christmas, was thought to ride across the frozen north to deliver winter presents to his followers. Odin, the Scandinavian equivalent of Woden, was a similar gift-bringer, rewarding the good and punishing the bad.

It was not until the Victorian period in Britain that gifts gradually came to be given on Christmas Day, and the custom developed from the idea that the infant Jesus delivered presents. It was also during this time that the story of Father Christmas became more widely established and children became more and more the focus of the festivities. The gift-giving industry began, one might say, to snowball. Until this time grocers, butchers and confectioners were more likely to benefit from the Christmas festival than toy makers.

New Year greetings cards were produced from engravings as early as the fifteenth century and it was common to write letters on decorated notepaper to friends and relatives at this time. The first Christmas card appeared in 1843, and the idea caught on rapidly as it saved all the time-consuming letter writing.

Opposite: There are some beautiful gift wrapping papers available today – much of it in imitation of the highly decorative wrapping used in Victorian times. Lace and ribbon trimmings can enhance the effect delightfully, making the simplest gift a real pleasure to receive.

FATHER CHRISTMAS

While the Christian church took over many of the ancient customs associated with the midwinter feast, it did not do so wholesale. Many of the traditions had to be adapted to fit Christian rather than pagan ideas. So the pagan god Woden was replaced with the more respectable St Nicholas, and in time children were encouraged by their parents to leave notes for him on 6 December requesting their Christmas presents.

After the Protestant Reformation and the rejection of many "popish" ideas, the figure of St Nicholas gradually merged with a figure of good cheer who was known as "the Spirit of Christmas". Father Christmas, already known from mummers plays, was altogether a more pagan

Below: Some Victorian Christmas cards had a spiritual and moral theme but many were humorous or romantic, containing the festive elements we now expect of Christmas – plenty of snow, Father Christmas in his sleigh, laughing children, robins, holly, mistletoe and, of course, a Christmas tree.

Right: This figure of Father Christmas shows the more traditional German representation. Looking more like a gnome or goblin, this shows how far the image of Santa Claus has been developed. In America in particular, the alterations were mostly for commercial ends.

character, who in his early days bore a club, was crowned with prickly holly, wore his robe wide open to reveal his chest and had the rubicund looks of a heavy drinker.

Dutch settlers in America took with them the tradition of St Nicholas, calling him *Sinterklaas*. By 1880 the Americans had tidied this up and standardized it to Santa Claus, creating the rotund, bearded, lovable old man, who is fond of children, wears red and white clothes and travels by a reindeer-drawn sleigh.

A poem by Clement Clark Moore written in 1822 and called "A Visit from St Nicholas" provides a clear portrait of Father Christmas/Santa Claus and is the one that the Victorians took to their hearts.

Below: So powerful is the Father Christmas myth that every year thousands of children write to him, usually care of Toyland, Lapland or The North Pole, requesting their presents for Christmas.

Left: This Christmas card of 1905 portrays Santa Claus in a highly romantic way – a far cry from the club-wielding, alcohol-loving figure of the medieval mummer's plays.

This early twentieth-century Christmas card is a familiar, if rather sentimental one. Since 1862 when a robin first appeared on a Christmas card, the little bird, a distinctive sight in winter in Britain, has been one of the most popular subjects.

Above and opposite: The Victorian revival of Christmas was so thorough, with old and new customs existing happily side by side that the card manufacturers not only had a wide variety of motifs to choose from but also a choice of moods, ranging from hilarious to sombre.

He was dressed all in fur from his head to his foot,
And his clothes were all tarnished with ashes and soot;
A bundle of toys he had flung on his back,
And he looked like a pedlar just opening his pack.
His eyes how they twinkled! his dimples how merry!
His cheeks were like roses, his nose like a cherry;
His droll little mouth was drawn up in a bow,
And the beard on his chin was as white as the snow.
The stump of a pipe he held tight in his teeth,
And the smoke it encircled his head like a wreath.
He had a broad face, and a little round belly
That shook, when he laughed, like a bowl full of jelly.
He was chubby and plump, – a right jolly old elf –
And I laughed when I saw him, in spite of myself.

To the Victorians, Father Christmas, as they preferred to call him, was the perfect character by which to extol the virtues of family, good-will and charity. He was the epitome of the spirit of Christmas – full of laughter and joy, always kind and generous and, above all, kind and loving to children. His place in the festivities was assured.

CHRISTMAS CARDS

When the first Christmas card appeared in 1843 it was denounced by some because the design, showing a Victorian family party drinking to the health of an absent friend, was thought to encourage drunkenness and alcoholism. Yet now, for many of us, the season of goodwill really starts when the first card drops through the letter-box. It signals not only that Christmas is really upon us – and we still haven't done a thing! – but that we are remembered by far-flung relatives, old and dear friends and new acquaintances.

Above: Quilling or paper filigree is an ancient and delightful craft. Originally it was practised in Mediterranean countries in imitation of gold and silver filigree work. Using the most basic of materials, quilling can create pretty cards such as these which may be given at Christmas. A little practise with the craft can also produce unusual tree decorations and festive mobiles.

Left: Spiritual themes and religious stories have always been, and will always be, a major inspiration for Christmas card designers. For Christians, the essence of Christmas is the Nativity and every year sees evocative representations of the event.

Opposite: Handmade Christmas cards are very rewarding – both to make and to receive. This is a simple cross stitch design which can be mounted in a handmade card or in one of the many commercial ones available.

Above: The gift-bearing character of Father Christmas has evolved over the centuries as an amalgam of the pagan god, Odin and the Christian St Nicholas. By the late nineteenth century he had developed into a rotund, lovable character, a friend to all children. In America he became known as Santa Claus.

Above right: Legend says that when Jesus Christ was on his way to Calvary, a robin pulled a thorn from His crown in an attempt to ease the Saviour's pain. The blood from the wound dyed the bird's breast red.

Previous page: Centuries ago gifts given at the end-of-year celebrations were only small tokens to wish the recipient well for the coming year. By the end of the nineteenth century these mostly edible gifts, such as honey, fruit and cakes, had largely given way to useful gadgets and, most notably, a wide range of toys for children.

Opposite: Convinced Santa has been in the night, two little girls open their presents on Christmas morning. Many households leave a small "snack" for Santa – in Britain this is usually a mince pie and perhaps a glass of sherry, if he's lucky!

By 1880 the sending of cards was a common practice, encouraged by the availability of the penny post and improved printing techniques. Innocent contentment, mirth and, above all, good nature were more often than not the sentiments expressed on Victorian Christmas cards, particularly when they depicted the poor. At first, favourite designs were not, as might be expected, religious but more simple, cheerful images, such as holly and mistletoe, robins and snow.

Whether you make your own cards or buy some of the seemingly numberless commercial ones, the sentiments that you send with it are likely to be personal – a simple greeting, a chatty note, a brief record of the past year, a promise to meet soon. The Christmas card started out this way, with the sending of a few lines, a "Christmas piece" to friends and relatives, written on prepared sheets and decorated with borders and scrolls, rather resembling a Valentine card.

Whatever the size, design or message, however, Christmas cards have an unchanging quality. They convey the sender's good-will. Such a card may be the *only* communication between distant family or old friends throughout the whole year, but somehow it is enough to maintain contact. Christmas cards, whatever their initial reception, are important to us – why else do we choose them with such care? They mirror what we feel about the recipients and what we wish them to feel about us. It is not surprising that the Christmas card soon became a messenger of kind thoughts, friendly greetings and good-will, although the fact that it increasingly came to replace personal calls is a shame, and some people try to recapture some of the spirit of Christmas past by delivering personally at least some of the cards they send.

GIVING PRESENTS

All through the Middle Ages and until this century gifts given at Christmas-time were really only small tokens, such as sweetmeats, small

The Victorians were nothing if inventive when it came to present-giving. How many of us today would relish being given a fire extinguisher for a Christmas present?

Right: Attractive packaging enhances any gift. The Victorians delighted in "yule-traps" which consisted of disguising one present by hiding it in another, testing the cleverness of the recipient in discovering the trick.

toys, fruit, nuts, almanacs, Bibles, dainty pieces of needlework and books. In Victorian times gifts were valued more for being homemade than for size and expense. Many people today would prefer a return to this less expensive custom – especially when the bills start arriving in January. In the last century the gifts for girls might include dolls, dolls' houses, pin-cushions, trinkets, needle-cases and paint boxes. For boys there might be working models, boats, trains, toy soldiers, drums and games.

Today, the highlight of Christmas is the giving and receiving of presents and surely it must be the *best* time to be a child. No headaches over what to buy and no anxiety over how much it all costs, just an excited early rising, a colourful pile of presents at the bottom of the bed or around the tree and hours and hours of fun.

In Britain the joy of the occasion is heightened by the customs surrounding gift-giving. Children are encouraged to write a letter to Father Christmas to indicate what they want for Christmas. The Post Office receives thousands every year – all addressed to the North Pole or Lapland. In many households with children a mince pie and a drink of some kind is left by the fireplace for Father Christmas so that he can refresh himself once he has squeezed down the chimney with his sack of gifts.

Smaller gifts, probably closer in spirit to the original New Year tokens, are often put in a Christmas stocking, which is variously hung on the chimney breast or at the foot of the bed. The "big" presents, all gaily wrapped, tend to be clustered under the Christmas tree. When my sister, Janette, and I were children we were allowed to open our stockings as early as we wished, as long as it was not before midnight because Father Christmas wouldn't yet have been and preferably *after* 6 a.m. so as not to wake our parents too early! I can still remember how excited we were as we groped towards the

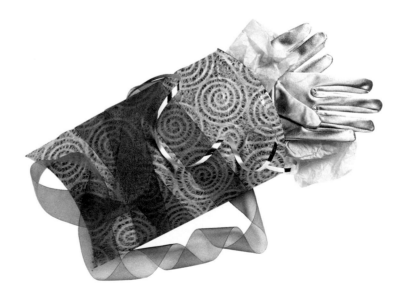

end of the bed to find the stockings there. "He's been! He's been!"

These customs vary from home to home, but they all add to the excitement of the occasion. Customs vary, too, from country to country. In Germany a beautiful girl wearing a crown of lighted candles and called the *Christkindl* leaves presents for children. She very cleverly leaves the gifts in

a locked room. The parents wake the children at midnight, unlock the room and there they are!

A friendly gnome called Julenisse, a sort of mini Santa Claus, delivers the presents during the night in many Scandinavian countries. A bowl of porridge instead of a mince pie is left out to help him on his way.

A little girl searching to the bottom of Santa's stocking is determined to find the last of her presents. Generally, Santa's stocking contains small gifts such as fruit, nuts, small colouring and story books, crayons and a selection box of sweets.

FEASTING AT CHRISTMAS

Right from its pagan origins, Christmas has always been a time of feasting. And what feasting! In the past the aim seemed to be to eat and drink as much as possible of as wide a range of things as possible! Meat formed the centrepiece of the festive table, and Christmas feasts of yesteryear included all manner of red and white meats, plus many types of fish. These ranged from the sublime to the ridiculous and included peacocks with gilded beaks, roast swans, boars' heads, haunches of venison, sides of roast beef and mutton, roast sucking pig, herb-stuffed pike, salmon, lobster, roast porpoise, carps' tongues, glazed hams, chicken and geese by the flock ...

Feasting was the major part of Christmas celebrations in medieval times. A vast array of meats were eaten, including swan, venison, suckling pig, beef, mutton, goose and many fish.

CHRISTMAS DAY DINNER

Christmas Day dinner has long been important not only because it celebrated the feast day itself but because it traditionally marked the end of the period of Catholic fasting through Advent. Meat was the main course, although the specific meats favoured varied from country to country. Spaniards prepared roast sucking pig; the Dutch preferred hare; the Germans and Austrians had goose; Icelanders favoured ptarmigan. Nations also tended to stay loyal to their traditional festive foods, taking their feasting customs with them when they settled in far-flung places, particularly the British, who took their preferences for turkey and plum pudding with them even to hot countries such as India and Australia.

Today, preparing for Christmas wining and dining is as important as buying the tree, decorating the house and wrapping the presents. Compared

Opposite: Plum or Christmas pudding is a wonderful sight, all aflame with brandy. The pudding actually evolved from a thick gruel called frumenty which was eaten during the fasting period before Christmas.

CHRISTMAS PAST

This delicious Christmas dinner of roast turkey and plum pudding is temptingly displayed on a table made festive with candles, crackers and mince pies.

with what was consumed in past centuries, however, we seem almost restrained in our eating habits. Certainly in Britain, Christmas dinner has perhaps become a rather stereotyped affair, with turkey, turkey and more turkey. It is worth remembering that turkey, like so much else of the Christmas we know, is a relatively recent arrival on our tables. In past centuries the list of avian fare alone that was available at Christmas-time was long and distinguished, with large quantities of birds imported from Europe. Considering all the poultry and game birds that were available – peacock, swan, lark, bustard, goose, duck, cockerel, chicken, capon, pheasant, partridge – and the fact that most of them are *still* available, it is surprising that turkey has taken over to such an overwhelming extent.

For centuries roast beef and goose were the most popular choices for the festive table, and traditionally goose was served on Michaelmas Day (29 September) and Christmas Day, with even the poorest families managing to have goose at Christmas. In Victorian times the "Goose Club" became popular, allowing less well-off families to save a small amount each week for several months so that they could afford their Christmas goose. In 1840, however, turkey was served for the first time at Queen Victoria's Christmas table, albeit on a side table, and by the 1850s it had supplanted the royal roast swan as the main dish. Its popularity with ordinary families

For centuries roast goose was the favourite dish for festive occasions. Traditionally it was served on Michaelmas Day (29 September). In the last century and much of this one, less well-off families saved up for their Christmas bird by regular contributions to the "Goose Club".

Opposite: By the 1850s, turkey had ousted roast swan as the centrepiece of Queen Victoria's Christmas table at Windsor. Its popularity was assured and for the general populace it increasingly replaced the goose that had traditionally been served.

Overleaf: A scrumptious array of cold pickles complement a succulent joint of ham. A cold table such as this was commonly served on Boxing Day, particularly in Britain.

Overleaf left: The round shape of Christmas pudding is due to the traditional method of cooking, which was to wrap it in a muslin cloth, tie the neck tightly with string and boil it for several hours.

Overleaf right: These festively decorated plum pudding sweetmeats would satisfy those with the sweetest of teeth. Christmas pudding has become so popular that the basic ingredients are now available in other foods, such as ice-cream, yogurts and truffles.

grew rapidly after this. By the middle of the nineteenth century it was a very popular dish at Christmas-time, and huge flocks of birds were driven from Norfolk to the London markets.

Turkeys were brought to Europe from the New World, and they were introduced to England from Spain during the sixteenth century. These ugly birds were given the name turkey because they were first brought to England by merchants from Turkey. Large-scale farming of the birds soon became established in Norfolk. Eating turkey at Christmas only, which we still largely do, is a relic of the days when everyone tried to have something special on the table during the festive season.

CHRISTMAS DESSERTS

Eating sweet things during the days of Christmas is a world-wide pleasure, and most European countries have some fascinating traditions in the making of cakes, breads, pies, pastries, biscuits, sweetmeats and puddings. Victorian England had a particularly sweet tooth and a large demand developed for, among other things, crystallized fruits, nougat, fudge, toffee, chocolate-covered nuts and marzipan fruits. Confectioners still find that Christmas is their best (most profitable) time of year. Certain puddings and sweetmeats have stood the test of time, such as plum or Christmas pudding and mince pies.

Rich and delicious Christmas pudding and brandy butter finish Christmas dinner in style. The Imperialistic fervour of the Victorians ensured that this traditional British pudding was imported all over the world. It was also the Victorians who began putting small coins and charms in the pudding.

CHRISTMAS PUDDING

Christmas pudding originally developed from a dish called frumenty, which was a sort of gruel eaten during the pre-Christmas fasting period. It was made of hulled wheat boiled in milk and seasoned with sugar and spices. Over the years, the recipe was thickened into a plum porridge by the addition of meat, breadcrumbs, eggs, prunes and spirits or ale. The traditional round shape resulted from the way it was cooked by being wrapped in a muslin cloth and boiled. By Victorian times the prunes had been replaced by sultanas and currants. It was also the Victorians who added the romantic notion of putting in lucky charms and small silver coins.

Recipes for Christmas pudding vary slightly even today but, the one that follows is similar to that eaten by Victorians and Edwardians.

> *12oz (350g) raisins*
> *6oz (175g) sultanas*
> *6oz (175g) currants*
> *3oz (85g) mixed peel*
> *3oz (85g) glacé cherries*
> *grated rind 1 lemon*
> *1oz (25g) ground almonds*
> *1/2 teaspoon mixed spice*
> *1/2 teaspoon grated nutmeg*
> *8oz (225g) brown sugar*
> *8oz (225g) suet*
> *8oz (225g) breadcrumbs*
> *4oz (115g) plain flour*
> *pinch salt*
> *4 medium eggs*
> *brandy*

Put all the dry ingredients into a large mixing bowl. Beat the eggs and stir in, adding sufficient brandy to moisten the mixture. Mix well, then transfer to a buttered bowl. Cover with a pudding cloth or piece of muslin and secure at the neck of the bowl with a string "handle". Steam for seven to eight hours, topping up the water in the steamer every so often. Once cooked, this pudding will keep for several months and will need another two hours' steaming to re-heat before serving (or microwave for a few minutes). It is most delicious served with brandy butter or thick cream.

MINCE PIES

Mince pies, like Christmas pudding, started off as a meat-based food, but eventually the meat was omitted and now only the suet remains. The shape of the pies has changed too. Originally they were oval, representing the shape of the crib of Jesus, and often the sunken lid contained a pastry form of the infant. The Puritans found such idolatry unacceptable, and mince pies were banned along with Christmas. Once Cromwell's rule in England was over, however, the pies re-emerged and took on a round shape.

Mince pies are only as good as the mincemeat used in them and home-made mincemeat is usually *far* tastier than that made commercially. Make the following mincemeat once and you'll be making it year after year – it's

simply delicious! The quantities given make about 4lb (1.8kg) of mince-meat (about two medium-sized jars). A jar of this mincemeat makes a wonderful gift at Christmas. Decorate the jar with a festive fabric top and a bright ribbon around the neck.

12oz (350g) raisins
12oz (350g) soft brown sugar
8oz (225g) sultanas
8oz (225g) currants
8oz (225g) mixed peel, finely cut (real fruit peel is by far the best)
8oz (225g) shredded suet (you could also use vegetarian suet)
1lb (450g) apples, peeled and chopped (use something with a bit of
* acidity, such as Granny Smiths or even Bramleys)*
4oz (115g) slivered almonds
juice and grated zest of 2 lemons
juice and grated zest of 2 oranges
4 level teaspoons mixed spice
1 level teaspoon powdered cinnamon
1/2 a grated nutmeg
6 tablespoons brandy

In 1895 The Woman at Home magazine suggested the following menu for Christmas dinner: hare soup, boiled turbot, roast beef, boiled turkey, mashed potatoes, broccoli, plum pudding, mince pies, raspberry trifle, biscuits, cheese, walnuts, dessert biscuits, French sweets and chocolate.

Preparing the Feast.

Mix all the ingredients (except the brandy) together in a large, oven-proof bowl then bake in a very cool oven at 110°C (225°F/gas mark ¼) for three hours. Remove from the oven and mix well. Allow to cool, then add the brandy and stir again. This mincemeat will keep well in air-tight containers for several months.

CHRISTMAS CAKE

The cake that we call Christmas cake – rich fruit cake covered with marzipan and royal icing and decorated with a Father Christmas figure and snow scene – is actually quite a modern tradition, dating from around the middle of the nineteenth century. Originally cake was served for afternoon tea on Twelfth Night (6 January), but Twelfth Night cake was a much grander affair, and was far more elaborately decorated. like a wedding cake.

Twelfth Night cake was traditionally baked in honour of the three kings who visited the baby Jesus, but by the late 1870s Twelfth Night or Epiphany had begun to die out as a separate feast day, so the inventive Victorians, requiring something suitable for Christmas afternoon tea, adapted the idea into what we now call Christmas cake.

"Christmas comes but once a year, and when it comes it brings good cheer."

Christmas Day dinner was doubly welcome in many households. Not only did it celebrate the feast day that was Christ's birth but it also marked the end of the traditional Catholic fasting during Advent.

Opposite: A hot toddy – perfect for frigid winter evenings, and especially welcome after attending a carol service in a draughty church.

CHRISTMAS CHEER

It will not be news to anyone that drinking has always been an important part of Christmas and New Year festivities. Toasting the gods, the sun, the earth, the soil, the plants, the animals – you name it – was a common and sensible custom centuries ago when mankind was at the mercy of so many potential natural disasters. Drink in all its many forms and "making merry" became a way of currying favour, giving thanks and celebrating the rebirth of spring and fertility.

From the Middle Ages drinking as part of wassailing was popular (see Chapter 3). The wassail bowl was taken from house to house, and the inhabitants toasted and invited to drink from the bowl. In return for the health toast, money was given, and drinks such as Lamb's Wool and mulled wine or ale were donated to refill the bowl.

LAMB'S WOOL

Lamb's wool was so-called because the apple pulp used in it looked like fuzzy wool. Bishop was a hot, spiced port wine much favoured by the Victorians as a more refined alternative to the lamb's wool in the wassail bowl.

4 dessert apples
3 tablespoons water
1/2 pt (300ml) sherry
2pt (1.2l) brown ale
3oz (85g) soft brown sugar
1/4 teaspoon grated nutmeg
1/4 teaspoon ground ginger
2in (5cm) piece cinnamon
strip of lemon peel

Core the apples, place them in an ovenproof dish with the water and bake for 20 minutes at 180°C (350°F/gas mark 4) or until soft. Remove from the oven, discard the peel and mash the apples in a bowl. Heat the sherry, ale, sugar, spices and lemon peel in a saucepan and keep on a low heat for about twenty minutes before transferring to a large, pre-heated serving or punch bowl. Stir in the warm apple and drink the wassail while hot.

MULLED WINE

Mulled or warmed wine or beer is a wonderful winter drink, ideal for chilly evenings. Gentle heating during preparation ensures that the alcohol does not evaporate. In the past a red-hot poker was used to warm the drink.

1 lemon
4 whole cloves
1pt (600ml) red wine
3oz (85g) soft brown sugar
4in (10cm) cinnamon stick
1/4 pt (150ml) brandy

Push the cloves into the lemon and put into a saucepan with the wine, sugar and cinnamon. Heat to simmering point, cover and simmer (do not boil) for two to four minutes. Remove from the heat, add the brandy, strain the drink and serve hot.

EGG WINE

In the last century, egg wine was drunk hot during outdoor activities such as skating. In a bowl beat two eggs with a little cold water. Bring one pint of spiced elder wine to the boil in a saucepan. Add the beaten egg to the wine, beating well until the mixture comes to the boil.

GAMES & PASTIMES

laying games has long been a feature of midwinter celebrations. In ancient Rome during Saturnalia gambling and dice games were allowed, sports competitions took place and plays were performed. The feast of Christmas, happily, includes the idea of having fun, and over the centuries many games and pastimes have developed, some of which still remain favourites.

One development of the last fifty years threatens to take over, however, for families today tend to watch many, many hours of television during the Christmas period. Such an exclusive and physically boring pursuit is difficult to understand when we consider the vast array of games available – and the fact that so many programmes and films screened over the Christmas holiday are making their second and even third appearance.

In previous centuries the period after Christmas dinner (which was eaten in the middle of the day) was a time for having fun and entering into the spirit of the party – no one wanted to sit around doing nothing. In fact, so much food was consumed during the Middle Ages that boisterous play was probably required to help the food go down in readiness for the next meal. In the time of Henry VIII games, particularly gambling games, were expressly forbidden at all other times of year except Christmas, so the games played then were long awaited and enjoyed with gusto.

Above and opposite: Celebrations of any kind usually mean fun and games. During Queen Victoria's reign, Christmas became much more a time for family, and children in particular. Games such as musical chairs, blind man's buff and hide and seek were simple to organise, lively and very popular at parties. Magazines of the late nineteenth century, such as Cassell's Family Magazine, would warn parents in a chivvying tone not to expect children to amuse themselves at parties. The boys would collect in one part of the room and probably conduct themselves roughly, while the girls would sit modestly and silently in another. Games organised by a grown-up person with energy and kindliness were suggested as the answer to this undesirable state of affairs.

The Victorians were very imaginative when it came to filling the hours over Christmas-time, taking their duties as parents and hosts very seriously. Many new games were introduced, but old favourites like blind man's buff were always popular. A more decorous version of the game was called shadow buff. In this quieter variation, the "blind man" would sit on one side of a white sheet or tablecloth which had a bright light shining on it. He or she would have to guess the identity of other players from the shadows they cast as they walked past the other side of the cloth.

INDOOR ENTERTAINMENTS

The French politician and gastronome Anthelme Brillat-Savarin (1755–1826) once said that to invite a person to your house is to take charge of his or her happiness while under your roof. The Victorians agreed with this sentiment and brought new life to entertainment and the fun and games at Christmas, especially when it came to indoor entertainment. The adults looked forward to soirées and balls and even some parlour games of their own, while the children had plenty of exuberant games to entertain them after the Christmas meals and enliven the parties that were common at that time of year.

Games such as snapdragon, hunt the slipper, hot cockles, hide and seek, musical chairs, Simon says, blind man's buff, the elements, Chinese whispers, the minister's cat and charades have long been popular, and many took on a new lease of life during the Victorian rejuvenation of Christmas. Children today, despite their tastes for computer games and television, also find them great fun. Keeping the customs alive is what makes Christmas such a special occasion, and it is a great shame that so many games have already been lost to history and are played no more – games like shoeing the wild mare, post and pair, puss in the corner and Rowland ho.

SNAPDRAGON

This very old game has long been a favourite, if rather hazardous, enjoyment at Christmas. It was reputedly invented by Hercules after he com-

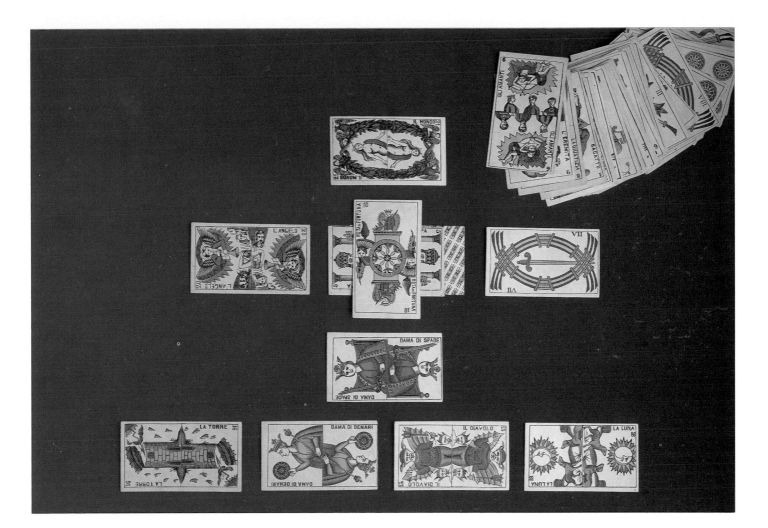

pleted his eleventh labour, slaying the dragon of Hesperides and making a fiery dish of the golden apples from the orchard.

Raisins or other dried fruit are piled into a shallow dish and well soaked with brandy. The brandy is then set alight and the room lights turned off. The participants then take turns in the eerie light to snatch the fruit from the burning dish, blow out the flames and eat it while the others sing an old rhyme.

Here he comes with flaming bowl,
Don't be mean to take his toll,
Snip! Snap! Dragon!

Take care you don't take too much,
Be not greedy in your clutch,
Snip! Snap! Dragon!

With his blue and lapping tonge
Many of you will be stung
Snip! Snap! Dragon!

For he snaps at all that comes,
Snatching at his feast of plums,
Snip! Snap! Dragon!

Indoor games might include tarot card readings. Despite their reputation for primness and piety, the Victorians enjoyed the thrill of something exciting – and what better than to have your fortune told.

Overleaf: The Victorians seemed to have a game for all ages and all occasions. Some needed nothing more than energy and enthusiasm. Others, like fancy dress, required props. Fancy dress costumes were de rigueur at many fashionable middle and upper class parties, with children dressed up in various guises. These included a page, a fishwife, a Moorish servant, a barrister, a Dutch woman, a jockey, a highwayman, a historical figure and any number of characters from fairy tales and nursery rhymes.

Right: A great many new industries sprang up in the second half of the nineteenth century to cope with the increased demand for games, particularly board games. Dominoes was popular, as was loto, a sort of early bingo. Bagatelle was a board game where small balls were fired by a spring-loaded mechanism into numbered holes, while spelicans or spillikins entailed picking thin wooden sticks from a pile of sticks without disturbing the rest.

Below: Charades has long been an ideal game for parties, best suited to older children and adults. It is great fun and a wonderful ice-breaker, even today.

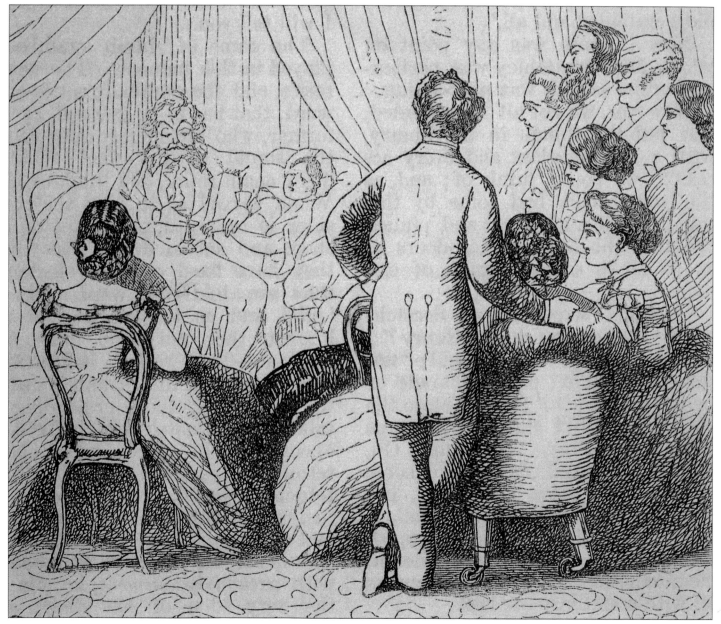

THE MINISTER'S CAT

This was a favourite Victorian game because it was not only educational but playable in polite circles. The players sit in a circle and the first person might say, "The Minister's cat is an angry cat". The next person in the circle might say, "The Minister's cat is an amazing cat", and so on until everyone has thought of an adjective beginning with A to describe the cat. Then everyone has to think of adjectives beginning with B, then C and so on, with the object being that no word is repeated.

CHARADES

This is one of the most popular of Christmas games and was greatly loved by the Victorians. The players are divided into teams and the first team has to think of a word or phrase, title of a book, poem, play, film, song, television or radio programme. This is then acted out in mime, often in syllables, until the full phrase is guessed.

If the weather was seasonal enough, with plenty of snow and freezing temperatures, there were thrilling outdoor pursuits to be enjoyed, such as tobogganing, snowball fights and ice skating.

Opposite above and below: Some games such as hopscotch, marbles, skittles and conkers have a timeless quality, handed down from generation to generation and enjoyed at any time of year.

Ice skating was a popular activity if the weather was seasonal but, if not, there were plenty of other entertainments available.

Above and opposite top: Sports and outdoor games make a welcome change, particularly on Boxing Day when everyone has had enough of over-eating and being cooped up in the house.

DUMB CRAMBO

To play this game, half of the players leave the room while the other half decide on a verb that the others have to guess. When the absent team returns they are told a word that rhymes with the one chosen. They consult and then, without words, have to act out what they think the word is. If their guess is wrong the other players hiss, if it is right, they applaud.

ADVERBS

The Victorians also delighted in acting or miming games, such as adverbs or "in the manner of the word" as it was often called. In this game a player is sent out of the room leaving the others to choose an adverb – a describing word such as awkwardly, happily, solemnly, drunkenly. The player then re-enters and requests other players to perform an action or mime "in the manner of the word" chosen – for example, they will be asked to read a book, eat a sandwich, stroll around the room. The player then has to guess the adverb that was chosen.

OTHER GAMES

Memory and magic games have also long been popular and are still great fun. Kim's memory game requires each player to have a pencil and piece of paper. A tray is then produced which has about twenty small objects on it, such as a teaspoon, holly leaf, comb, pencil and so on. The players study the contents for one minute, the tray is then removed, and they have to write down as many of the objects as they can remember. The winner is the one who remembers the most.

After the boisterous group games, a typical Victorian Christmas party

Below: Most British children would agree that there simply isn't enough snow at Christmas-time. A white Christmas cannot really be relied upon in Britain, particularly in the south of the country, so there is always great excitement when snow does arrive. Snowball fights, making snowmen, tobogganing and skating are all the more wonderful then.

would have the company sitting more quietly to listen to individual "party pieces" – this might be singing a song, doing a conjuring trick, playing the harp or piano, reciting a poem or telling a story. Finally, after all these solo entertainments everyone would come together again around the piano and sing songs and carols.

OUTDOOR ENTERTAINMENTS

The range of outdoor games and entertainments enjoyed in the past, and even today to some extent, often depended on the weather. Decent falls of snow meant that games such as making a snowman, ice skating and tobogganing were possible.

More kindly weather allowed for all manner of sports, such as riding, hunting, archery and kite flying. Organized entertainment would include attending plays, ballet and pantomimes.

Today each country has its own favourite outdoor activities during the Christmas season. For example, in Canada there are the traditional winter sports of skiing, ice hockey, skating, curling and tobogganing. In contrast, an Australian Christmas is characterized by swimming, surfing and cricket, with the start of the Sydney to Hobart yacht race taking place on Boxing Day. In Britain there is horse racing, the Boxing Day hunt and many football (soccer) fixtures.

THE PANTOMIME

Mime, or silent drama, dates from ancient times, but going to a pantomime at Christmas-time is still a hugely popular pastime. The traditional characters in a pantomime, for example, Columbine and Harlequin, came from a sixteenth-century Italian form of comedy, *commedia dell'arte*. From this evolved the harlequinade of the early eighteenth century. This was a brief sketch, usually based on a classical fable and often humorous. The sketches were generally mimed and were meant to keep the audience entertained between the acts of a play. Gradually these sketches became longer and more sophisticated.

It was the Victorians who popularized pantomimes, and Christmas became *the* season for their performance. The Victorians disapproved of the bawdy antics of Harlequin, and his escapades were gradually replaced by more harmless fun, enacted through jolly fairy tales and nursery rhymes. The tradition of having a male dame and a female principal boy dates back to the Roman Saturnalia and the medieval Lord of Misrule, where topsy-turvy role play was common. Sadly, that custom seems to be dying out somewhat today.

British pantomimes today are no longer dumb shows but a great family event, with children in particular loving the chaos, the interactive elements and over-the-topness of it all. With their sense of fun – "Oh yes he is!" "Oh no he isn't!" – and spirit of make-believe, pantomimes epitomize Christmas, and shows such as *Aladdin, Puss in Boots, Cinderella* and *Dick Whittington* are perennial favourites with their elaborate fairy-tale fantasies, showy scenery, topical allusions and jokes, popular songs and general buffoonery.

INDEX

(Page references in *italics* denote illustrations)

Hanukkah (Chanukah) (*see* Feast of Lights)
Henry VIII, 113
holly, *17*, 45, 47, *52* (*see also* evergreens)

Illustrated London News, The, 23
industrialization, 30
ivy, 45, 49 (*see also* evergreens)

Jews, 13
Julenisse, 87
Juvenalia, festival of, 11

Kalendae Januarii, 11, 75
kissing bough, 65

Lord of Misrule, 13–14, *14*, *16*, 17, 124

Middle Ages, 13, 84, 109, 113
midnight mass, 43
mince pies, 99, 102

mistletoe, *17*, 45, 49 (*see also* evergreens)
Mithras, 11
mummer's play, *14*, 14–15, 76
musical chairs,

Nativity, the, 6, *10*, *11*, *12*
New Year, 35, 37, 75, 86

Odin, 75

pagan, 11, 13, 14, *17*, 35
pantomime, 124
paper decorations (*see* Christmas decorations)
pastimes, *26*, 36, 111–124
Pickwick Papers, The, 26–7, 30
plum pudding (*see* Christmas pudding)
presents, *22*, *23*, *29*, *31*, 64, 73, 82–3, 84–7, 86, 87
Prince Albert, 21, *22*, 22–3, 61
Puritans, 17, 21, 102

robin, *78*, 84
roles, exchanging, 11, 14, *16*
Roman Church, 13
Romans, 11, *23*, 45, 75
royal icing, 105

Santa Claus, 21, 77, *77*, 85, 87 (*see also* Father Christmas)
Saturn, 11
Saturnalia, festival of, 11, 45, 113, 124
Sinterklaas, 77
St Nicholas, 21, 76
Stir-up Sunday, 41, *41*
superstitions, 43, 47, 49, 59

Thor, 13, 35
traditions, 33–43
turkey, 21, *43*, 94, 95–8
Twelfth Night cake, 105

Victoria, Queen, 7, 21, *22*, 22–3, 39, 75, 95
Vikings, 11, 35

wassail, wassailing, 13, 37, 39, 109
wassail bowl, 37, 42, 109
Wodan, 75, 76
wrapping paper, *74*, 86

yule, 35, *35*
yule-log, 35, *35*, 36

PICTURE CREDITS